Literature on the Move

Literature on the Move

Making and Using Pop-Up and Lift-Flap Books

Gerry Bohning

Ann Phillips

Sandra Bryant

Illustrated by
Sandra Bryant

1993
Teacher Ideas Press
A Division of
Libraries Unlimited, Inc.
Englewood, Colorado

Dedicated to the students at Barry University
and Lincoln Park Academy and to Paula, Cliff, and Kevin

TEACHER IDEAS PRESS
A Division of
Libraries Unlimited, Inc.
P.O. Box 6633
Englewood, CO 80155-6633

Library of Congress Cataloging-in-Publication Data

Bohning, Gerry.
    Literature on the move : making and using pop-up and lift-flap books / Gerry Bohning, Ann Phillips, Sandra Bryant ; illustrated by Sandra Bryant.
    vii, 116 p. 22x28 cm.
    Includes index.
    ISBN 1-56308-070-2
    1. Toy and movable books--Design. 2. Creative activities and seat work. 3. Language arts (Elementary) 4. Cut-out craft.
I. Phillips, Ann, 1941- . II. Bryant, Sandra. III. Title.
Z116.A3B55 1993
736'.98--dc20
    92-35192
    CIP

Contents

Introduction

Pop-up and lift-flap books are full of surprises. The books link a marvel of movement with the story through the real movement of lift-flaps, pull-tabs, fold-a-frames, accordion folds, turn wheels, springs, V pop-ups, moving mouths, or other paper actions. These moving picture books are fun to make and fun to read. The process of book production—planning, writing, editing, drawing, and assembling—helps children understand plot and story structure.

The technical aspects of making the paper actions for pop-up and lift-flap books are not complicated. Chapter 1 of this guide offers directions for making eight basic movable shapes for books. Variations of each shape are included so teachers and students can make a number of figures from a single basic shape. The paper action shapes are illustrated in an easy to follow step-by-step format using classroom examples. "Ways to Put Books Together" is at the end of chapter 1. This section includes ideas that students can use to assemble individual or class books.

Chapter 2 offers creative thematic ideas that teachers can use to make moving picture books an integral part of reading and writing to reinforce curriculum area concepts. Pop-up and lift-flap curriculum projects are organized by category for easy thematic teaching: folklore, holidays, family and friends, animals, word fun, biographies, our earth, transportation, and sports. Each thematic unit includes children's books that can be used as springboards for reading and writing projects. Directions are given to guide the teacher and the students.

Creative teachers look for ways to excite children about reading and writing. Pop-up and lift-flap books appeal to all children. Children become excited when they develop their own movements to carry out the sequence of a favorite story or one that they write. Children can work alone or as a group to assemble an individual or class book. The actions invite repeated use of their new book. Not only do children enjoy reading their own book over and over, but also they find equal delight in reading a classmate's book. Children also enjoy sharing their books with their families, which encourages stretching learning beyond the confines of the classroom.

1 | Paper Actions and Bookmaking

LIFT-FLAPS

Lift-flaps offer the pleasure of a surprise and the challenge of proving a prediction. Lift the flap to find a baby chick hatching, a frog eating insects, or a puppy in a magician's hat. You might even find the answer to a riddle. Easy to make for even the youngest learner, lift-flaps can be made for a class book or as an individual project. Four basic action designs are described for making and using lift-flaps:

- Easy lift-flaps

- H-frame lift-flaps

- Shaped lift-flaps

- Picture lift-flaps

Using lift-flaps will help carry out your teaching objective, and will create high involvement and excitement in reading, writing, and sharing.

Easy Lift-Flaps

1. Tape, staple, or glue a paper flap to a large sheet of construction paper. Attach only the top edge of the flap. The flap may be any size.

2. Illustrate and color the lift-flap and the area under the lift-flap.

3. Create some flaps to open at the side by attaching one side instead of the top.

Outside flap: Haunted House

4. Add more than one lift-flap to a page.

H-Frame Lift-Flaps

1. Fold in half a 12"-x-18" sheet of construction paper. Crease. Open the paper and cut a letter *H*.

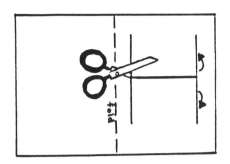

2. Fold the top flap up and the bottom flap down.

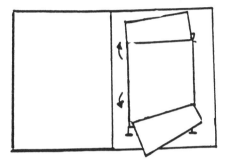

3. Refold the paper along the half crease so that the H-frame is on top and the flaps are facing out. Glue the paper along the top, side, and bottom.

   Draw and color illustrations. Write an accompanying story or report.

4. Follow steps 1-3 but turn the paper horizontally for a window lift-flap.

Shaped Lift-Flaps

1. Select a large sheet of
    construction paper.

    Using another sheet of paper,
    cut a flap in any shape.

    Glue or staple the flap to
    the large sheet of paper.

2. Illustrate and color the
    page.

Outside: green leaf

Outside: black hat

Picture Lift-Flaps

1. Select a large sheet of construction paper.

    Using either of the lift-flap actions already described, make the lift-flap an integral part of an entire scene.

An alligator is under the log lift-flap.

2. Lift-flaps can be combined with written work for stories and reports.

This is a good follow-up to a lesson on eggs and chicks.

PULL-TABS

Pull-tabs are paper handles that initiate movement through slits in the page. A pull-tab can bring a Halloween bat near the moon or return a busy bee to the hive to store nectar gathered from the flowers. Three basic action designs are described for making and using pull-tabs:

- Slide-tabs

- Slot-tabs

- Pivot-tabs

Is that a clown on a unicycle trying to balance on a tightwire? Give the pull-tab a tug and see whether she makes it across the wire or falls in the tub of water below!

Slide-Tabs

1. Cut two strips from tagboard or a file folder. Make the strips about 1" wide and about 9" long. Glue the strips together. This is the slide.

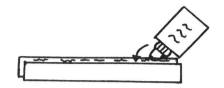

2. Cut another strip 1" wide and 5" long. Fold in half. This is the tab. Fold the tab end over the slide strip and glue or staple the tab and the slide together.

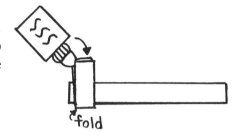

3. Fold in half a sheet of 12"-x-18" construction paper.

   Open the paper.

   Cut a diagonal slit for the tab path about 4" or 5" long.

   Cut a set of slits near the page edge a little over 1" long for the slide strip to fit through. The two smaller slits should start even with the top of the big diagonal slit.

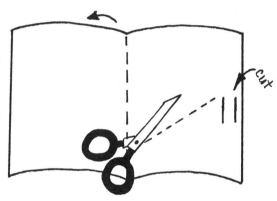

4. Insert the slide tab.

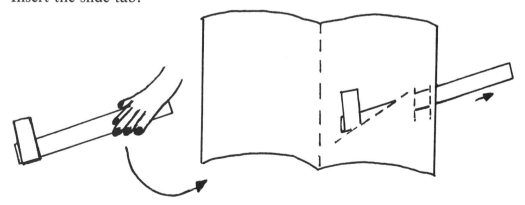

5. Fold in half another sheet of construction paper. Refold the slide-tab page and insert in the folded sheet of construction paper. Glue the construction sheet to the back of the slide tab page for support. Do not glue near the slits or the slide tab.

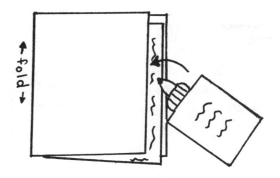

6. Draw, color, and cut out the figure to be glued to the tab.

7. Put a dab of glue on the tab and glue the figure to the tab. Remember to always put glue on the tab rather than on the figure. Complete the illustrations for the story or report. Caution readers to pull the tab out before the page is closed so that the figure does not get bent.

Slot-Tabs

1. Cut two strips from tagboard or a file folder about 1" wide and 9" long. Glue the two strips together.

2. Fold in half a sheet of 12"-x-18" construction paper.

   Open the paper.

   Cut slots a little over 1" wide and 1" long for the pull-tab. Cut one slot at the top and two slots at the bottom so the tab is at the back of the paper. Place the slots on the page to suit the planned picture.

3. Insert the pull-tab.

   Fold and glue another sheet of construction paper to the back of the page for support. Do not get glue on the pull-tab.

4. Draw, color, and cut out the figure to be attached to the pull-tab. Put a dab of glue on the pull-tab and glue the figure to the pull-tab. Complete the illustrations for the story or report. The tab can be shortened to suit the picture or report.

Pivot-Tabs

1. Use a 12"-x-18" sheet of construction paper.

   Cut an arc slit where you want the picture to move.

   Cut a circle near the page bottom about 1" diameter.

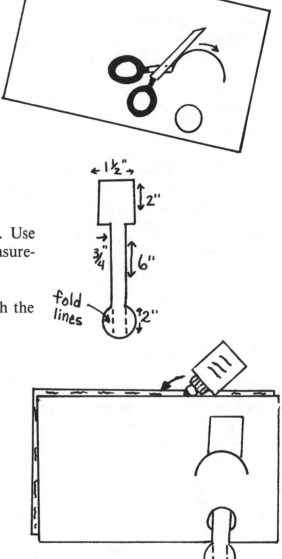

2. Make a pivot-tab shaped like a paddle. Use tagboard or a file folder. The pictured measurements are suggested.

   Fold the bottom flaps so they fit through the circle you cut in the construction paper.

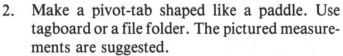

3. Insert the pivot-tab through the circle and the arc-slit. Unfold the bottom flaps of the pivot-tab so the pivot stays in place.

   Glue a second sheet of construction paper to the page back for support. Do not glue near the pivot.

4. A picture can be drawn on the pivot-tab or drawn separately, cut out, and pasted to the tab. Complete the pivot illustration and the story or report.

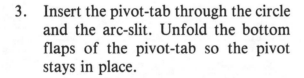

FOLD-A-FRAMES

Two cuts and a push and you have a fold-a-frame. Fold-a-frames are sturdy supports that hold figures related to a story or report. When the page is opened, the figure stands up. Probably the most adaptable of all the action designs, a fold-a-frame can hold one or several pop-up objects, depending on how many are needed to carry out a child's creative idea. Four basic action designs are described for making and using fold-a-frames:

- Cut frames

- Box frames

- Picture frames

- Cage frames

Comparison and contrast pictures, life on a farm, or reptiles in the Everglades all can be brought to three-dimensional life with fold-a-frames.

Cut Frames

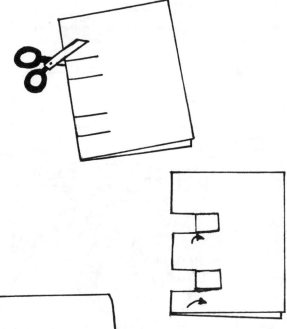

1. Fold in half a 12"-x-18" sheet of construction paper. File folders also work well.

    Cut two sets of slits about 2" long and fold back the flaps. The sets do not have to be the same width or the same length.

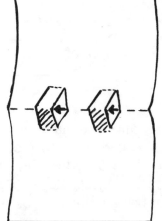

2. Open the paper.

    Pinch the crease in the middle of each flap and pull the flaps forward.

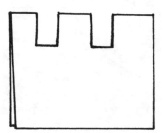

    As you pull the crease forward, fold the paper in half again so it looks like this.

    The flaps will be tucked inside.

3. Open the paper.

Complete the page by drawing, coloring, and cutting out pictures to put on the tabs. Put a dab of glue on each tab and glue the pictures to the tabs. Remember to always put glue on the tab rather than the picture. Write the story or report for the page.

4. Fold and glue another sheet of construction paper to the back of the page for support.

Any number of slots can be used for the frames.

Box Frames

1. Cut a strip of construction paper about 2" wide and 8" long. Fold in half. Fold in half again.

2. Unfold the strip and refold on the creases to make a cube shape.

3. Fold in half a 12"-x-18" sheet of construction paper.

   Open.

   Glue the back and bottom of the cube to the paper. Use as many cubes as needed.

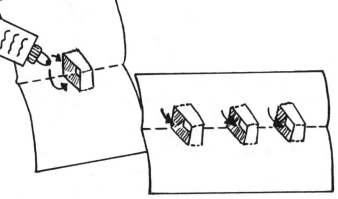

4. Draw, color, and cut out pictures for the cubes. Put a dab of glue on the front of each cube and glue the pictures on. Finish the illustrations and the story or report. Fold and glue another sheet of construction paper to the back of the page for support.

Picture Frames

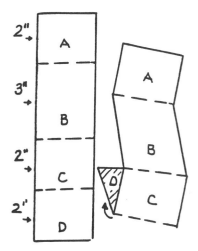

1. Cut a strip of construction paper about 3" wide and 9" long. Crease folds for the four sections as shown.

2. Illustrate the strip.

   The D section is the bottom and is not illustrated.

3. Fold in half a 12"-x-18" sheet of construction paper.

   Open the paper and glue the picture frame to the paper. Finish the illustrations. Fold and glue another sheet of construction paper to the back of the page for support.

   Complete the story or report.

Cage Frames

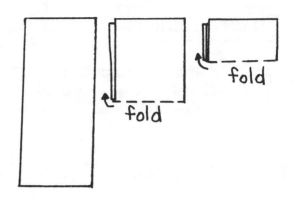

1. Cut a strip of construction paper about 4" wide and 9" long. Fold in half. Fold in half again.

2. Unfold the second fold only.

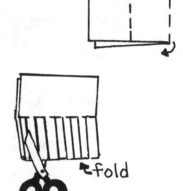

3. Cut cage bar slits to the crease of the second fold.

   Make sure there are an uneven number of strips.

4. Fold up every other strip. Cut off the strips that are folded up. This makes for easy viewing through the cage.

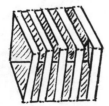

5. Refold as a cube.

6. Fold down one-third of a 12"-x-18" sheet of construction paper.

Open.

Glue the back and bottom of the cage cube to the paper at the fold.

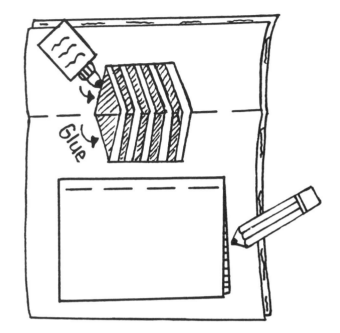

The cage can be a cage, crate, tower, fence, or other structure. Complete the illustrations and the story or report for the page.

A figure can be glued inside the cage by leaving a tab on the figure bottom and then folding the tab and gluing the tab to the page.

Fold and glue another sheet of construction paper to the back of the page for support.

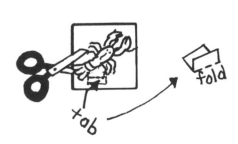

ACCORDION FOLDS

Accordion folds are a string of folded silhouettes that march into action as the page is opened. Simple silhouettes are cut out and the details are added with crayons or coloring pens. For example, where there is one car for a train, there are sure to be others. A string of connecting rectangles can quickly become the train cars, complete with engine and caboose. Connecting circles can become beach balls, and semicircles can form a color array for the rainbow. Accordion folds add movement as well as a three-dimensional feature. Using accordion folds to accompany stories and reports invites participation. Stories and reports may be stapled or glued to the top or bottom of a page; extra pages also may be taped on. Who can resist opening the page to find out what pleasure lies in wait?

1. Cut a strip of paper 3" or 4" wide and 9" long.

   Fold in half. Fold in half again.

fold

double fold

2. Draw an outline of a figure so that the top and bottom of the figure are oriented toward the unfolded edges.

   The figure must have tabs or limbs that touch the sides of the paper; these connect the accordion folds together.

double fold

double fold

tab

3. Cut around the figure. *Do not* cut the fold, as this connects the figures. Unfold. Draw the details on each figure and color.

fold

color

4. Fold in half a 9"-x-12" sheet of construction paper.

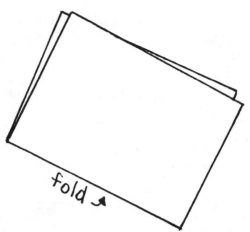

5. Open the paper and lay the folded figures across the page. The two middle figures need to be placed so the fold crease is out toward you.

   Glue *under* the left figure on the left side of the page.

6. Glue *under* the right figure on the right side of the page.

7. Close the paper.

Make sure the two middle figures are pulled toward you as you fold the paper so they meet; they will then pop out when the page is opened.

8. Wait until the glue has had time to dry thoroughly. Open the page.

9. Complete the rest of the illustrations.

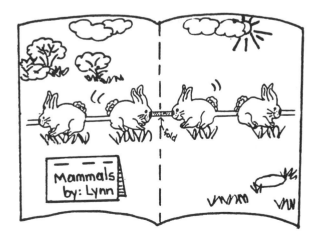

10. Add the story or report by gluing or stapling it to the page. Additional pages may be added.

TURN WHEELS

Tadpoles hatch, a shark swims in the ocean, and flowers are watered, all with the turn of a paper wheel. Turn wheels enhance the pleasure of writing and sharing because they invite participation. A scene on a wheel is the perfect action for adding vegetables to make stone soup or to watch the seasons change. Three basic action designs are described for making and using turn wheels:

- Shaped wheels

- Windows and wheels

- Picture wheels

Each will stimulate imagination and turn a story or report into an exciting writing adventure that is sure to be shared with classmates, friends, and family.

Shaped Wheels

1. Fold a 9"-x-12" sheet of construction paper so about one-third of it is folded up.

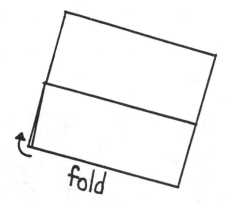

2. Cut a wheel from another sheet of construction paper or from tagboard so that it fits about half in and half out of the fold pocket. Tracing around a lid works well.

   Assemble with a brass fastener.

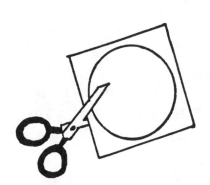 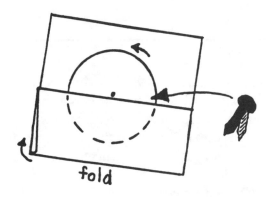

3. Remove brass fastener so you can finish working on the wheel on a flat surface. Draw and color what is to go on the wheel. Cut around the top of the figures. Draw and color the background to complete the scene. Reassemble the wheel and staple the sides of the pocket flap.

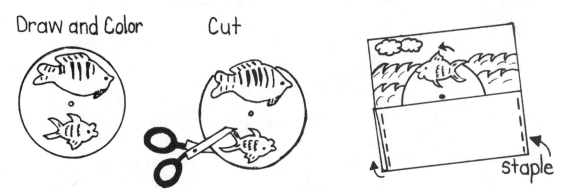

4. Add the report as a lift-flap glued on the front or back. You might also attach another page for the report.

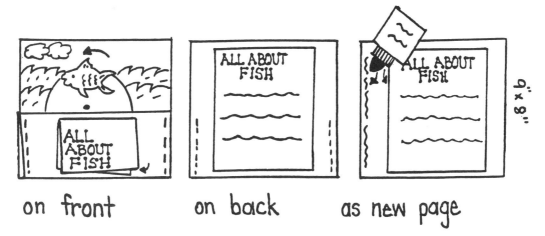

on front   on back   as new page

5. The fold may be at the top of the page instead. The wheel will still be attached to the middle of the page.

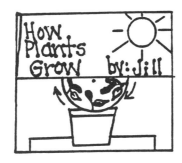

Windows and Wheels

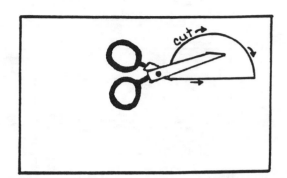

1. Cut out a half-circle window in a 12"-x-18" sheet of construction paper.

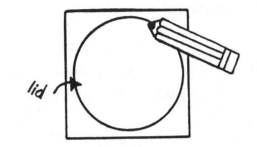

2. Use a large lid to trace a circle on a piece of tagboard or a file folder. The circle must be bigger than the window in the sheet of paper. Cut out the circle.

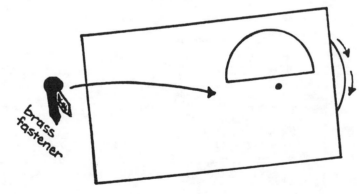

3. Use a brass fastener and assemble the circle behind the window so part of the wheel sticks out on the edge for easy turning.

4. After students have the idea of the wheel "fit," they usually prefer to take out the brass fastener so they can work on the wheel on a flat surface for the illustrations. The wheel is then reassembled and the story or report stapled to the paper.

5. Glue a sheet of construction paper to the back of the page to give support. Be careful not to get glue on the wheel.

6. Illustrate all around the window so it becomes part of the total picture.

7. The window also can be placed near the bottom of the page.

8. Window pages also can be made with a quarter-circle window. This gives four scenes for a sequence for the wheel.

   Follow the same basic assembly but use a quarter-circle window.

examples for quarter-circle turn wheels

Picture Wheels

1. Fold a 12"-x-18" sheet of construction paper.

   Cut out the wheel from tagboard the size to suit the purpose. All of the wheel is intended to be in view for a picture wheel.

   Assemble with a brass fastener.

2. Complete the illustrations.

   The story or report is glued inside.

SPRINGS

Springs do all sorts of interesting jobs. They help rope cattle for cowboys, send off rockets with a fiery blast of power, or provide the leash for walking a pet dog. On a more relaxed day, springs serve as the fishline so that the big one doesn't get away. Springs will even help butterflies flutter from the page. Two basic action designs are described for making and using springs:

- Coiled springs

- Folded springs

Both are easy to make paper actions that give reading and writing a surprise for every page.

Coiled Springs

1. Draw a spiral on a sheet of paper. Make the coils wide enough to draw on them if needed. The size of the coil depends on the size of the entire picture.

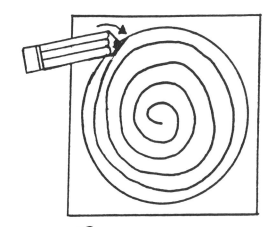

2. Draw what the coil is to be and color it. Also color the back if needed. Often it is not necessary to draw or color the coil. For example, if the coil is to be a rope, you could draw your spiral on a sheet of brown paper.

snake

fireman's hose

3. Cut out the coil.

4. Fold in half a sheet of 12"-x-18" construction paper.

fold

5. Open the paper and put the coil on the left side of the page. The paper also can be opened at the top and the coil placed on the upper part.

    Place a little glue *under* the coil at point A.

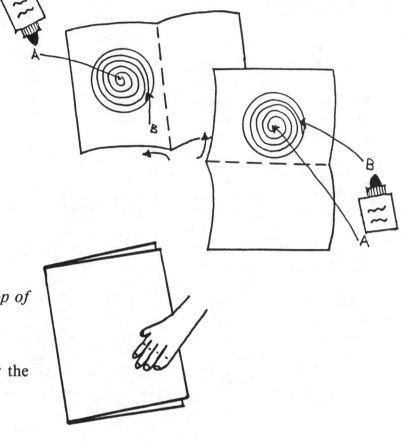

6. Place a little glue *on top of* the coil at point B.

    Close the paper. Allow the glue to dry.

7. Open. Complete the rest of the illustrations for the story or report.

8. Two smaller coils can be used on one page.

9. Coil pages also can be stapled to a larger sheet so there is room for the story or report.

Folded Springs

1. Cut two strips of paper about ½" wide and 4" long. Glue the strips together to form an L shape. Wait for the glue to dry.

2. Fold the strip into a spring. The bottom of the L shape is folded to the left first and the top is then folded down. Continue doing this same fold pattern until the whole strip is folded.

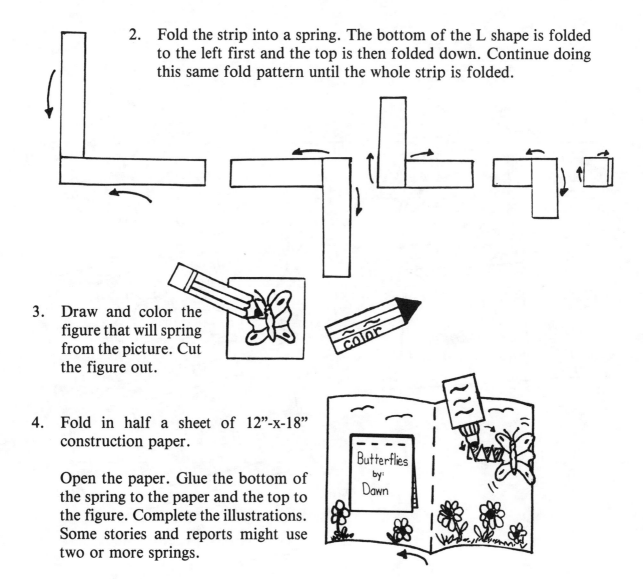

3. Draw and color the figure that will spring from the picture. Cut the figure out.

4. Fold in half a sheet of 12"-x-18" construction paper.

   Open the paper. Glue the bottom of the spring to the paper and the top to the figure. Complete the illustrations. Some stories and reports might use two or more springs.

V POP-UPS

V pop-ups can fling a kite into the air, bring a castle into view, send a mother bird to her nest, or show Cinderella's wicked stepmother. V pop-ups offer young writers a way to bring action to their story characters and movement to the scenes. Folding and pasting is all that is needed. V pop-ups are favorites for holiday story scenes—a jack-o-lantern can frighten the most cautious reader, to the delight of the student who made the scary book! Three basic action V pop-ups are described:

- Surprise V pop-ups

- Nose V pop-ups

- Folded V pop-ups

Each offers clever movements, and each helps motivate students to read and write.

Surprise V Pop-Ups

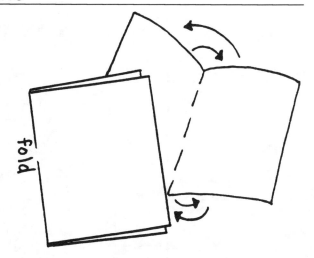

1. Fold in half a 9"-x-12" sheet of construction paper. Fold the paper back and forth several times so the fold hinge is very loose.

2. Fold down the corner about 2" at the folded edge.

    Fold the flap back and forth several times, front to back and back to front. The flap also must have a loose fold hinge.

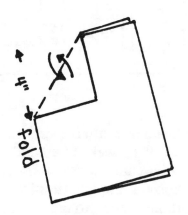

3. Open the sheet.

    Pull the triangle of the folded flap toward you at point A.

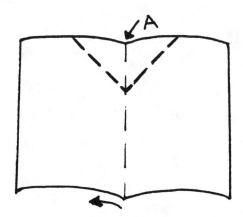

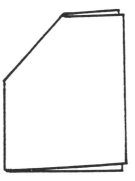

4. As the triangle comes toward you, close the paper, with the folded V on the inside.

5. Open the page to draw the illustrations.

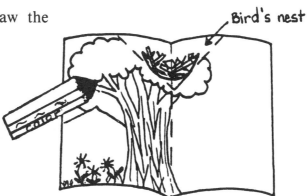

Bird's nest

6. On a 3" or 4" square of construction paper, draw the figure that is to pop up.

7. Color and cut out the figure.

    Fold the figure in half so the coloring is to the inside.

    Put the glue on the fold line on the side not colored.

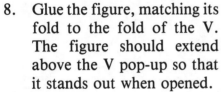

8. Glue the figure, matching its fold to the fold of the V. The figure should extend above the V pop-up so that it stands out when opened.

    The story or report is glued to the page.

    Fold in half another sheet of construction paper and glue it to the back of the page for support.

Nose V Pop-Ups

1. Fold the same steps as steps 1 and 2 for Surprise V Pop-Ups (page 36).

2. Turn the paper so the V fold is at the bottom.

   To make a nose, cut to the crease and down.

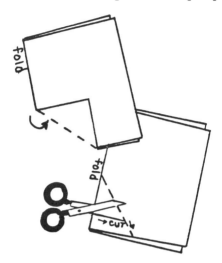

3. Open the page.

   Pull the triangle up toward you at point A.

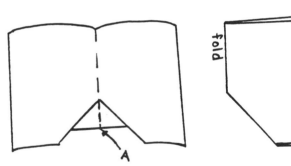

   As the triangle comes toward you, close the paper with the folded V on the inside.

4. Fold in half a sheet of construction paper and glue on the back. The back sheet provides paper for the mouth and chin.

   Open the page and complete the illustrations for the story or report.

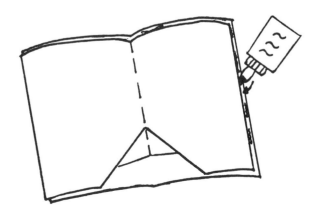

Folded V Pop-Ups

1. Fold in half a strip about 3" wide and 8" long.

Cut a *V* out at the center fold. Cut about 1" into the strip.

2. Fold back the bottom for the glue tab.

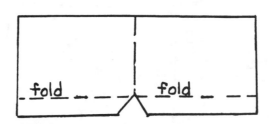

Draw and color the strip to suit the story or report.

3. Fold in half a 9"-x-12" sheet of construction paper.

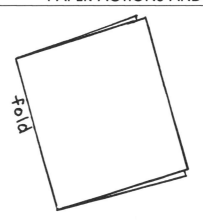

Open the page and color the scenery.

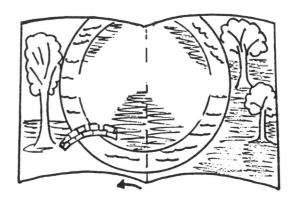

4. Glue the tabs of the strip to the paper in a V shape.

glue tabs

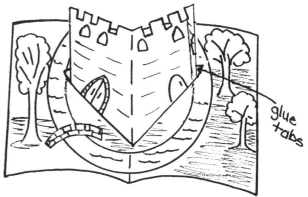

glue tabs

MOVING MOUTHS

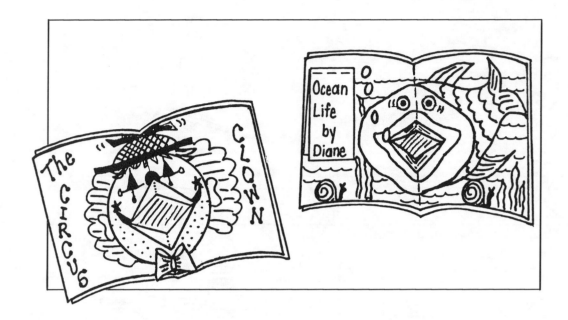

Moving mouth actions are simple to make and always invite a good conversation for verbal language development. A moving mouth can be a talking ghost, a fire-breathing dragon, a gulping fish, or a baby chick. An alligator might even come snapping out of the Florida Everglades! A moving mouth brings a story character alive for a student. Writing takes on a personal dimension with a moving mouth. A few easy folds and the action will all be in the mouth!

1. Fold in half a 9"-x-12" sheet of construction paper.

    Cut a slit about 2" long where the mouth is to be.

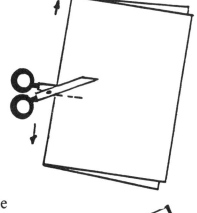

2. Fold the slit to make triangle flaps. Fold the flaps back and forth several times, from front to back and back to front. It is very important to have loose fold hinges.

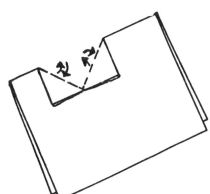

3. Open the paper.

    Pull up and back on points A and B.

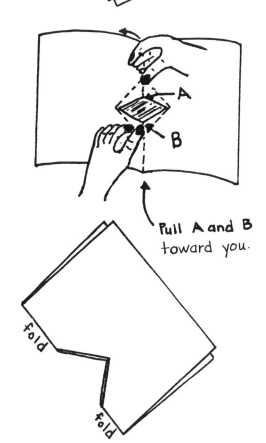

Pull A and B toward you.

4. As the points come together, fold the paper to look like this:

    The mouth will be inside the paper.

5. Open the paper.

   Illustrate the story or report.

6. Fold in half another sheet of construction paper and glue to the back of the page for support. Do not get glue near the moving mouth.

   A paper or ribbon tongue can be added by gluing it inside the mouth to the back sheet.

WAYS TO PUT BOOKS TOGETHER

The pride of having written a book is evident by a student's obvious delight in sharing the book again and again. Every book is award-winning to a child — an award of, "This is *my* book."

Bookbinding turns separate pages into a complete book. Books can be put together with staples, tape, fasteners, laces, rings, spiral bindings, or cloth. Students enjoy decorating the front covers and then putting the book together and binding it. Covers may be laminated or covered with clear contact paper to make them more attractive and durable.

Children prize their individual or class books. Gather up the pages and let's go to press!

The Front Pages

Pages can be prepared at the beginning to follow the format of a published book.

Dedication

To my bike.
It was the
model for my
story.

Dedication Page

Copyright 1992
Barry School

Copyright Page

"

My New Bike

by:

Christopher

Title Page

If the book has "chapters," a table of contents can be included.

Table of Contents
Page
I. My Wish 2
II. The Surprise 4

The Back Pages

Pages also can be added at the end of the book.

Rachael Maxwell

My name is
Rachael. I am
9 years old. I
have been
writing books
all year. I write
riddles.

Biography Page

Rachael,
This is a good
story.
Ms. Merry

Rachael,
I like the
pictures. Kevin

Rachael,
I love it! Mom

Readers Page

Readers
write their
comments about
the book.

The Front and Back Covers

A wide variety of materials work well for the covers. Use whatever is available and whatever the students can bring from home.

- Construction paper
- Tagboard or file folders
- Cardboard from tables or boxes

- Contact paper
- Wallpaper
- Cloth

A front cover is a very personal part of the book. Children like to make it special with their illustrations and artwork. Various art techniques such as the following help make the cover attractive.

- Spatter painting
- Collage
- Crayon etching
- Watercolors
- Finger painting
- Sponge painting

- Chalk
- Pasted tissue paper
- Photographs
- Real miniature objects
- Paper ceramic tiles
- Ribbon/string/yarn

Binding Books

Staples. Staple the pages and cover together. Use colored tape or masking tape to cover the staples. This makes the binding sturdier and more appealing.

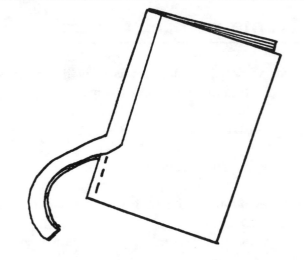

Brass Fasteners. Punch holes through the pages and covers. Use brass fasteners as the binding.

Rings. Punch holes through the pages and covers, either at the top or at the side.

Use notebook rings, curtain or shower rings, or old keyrings as the binding.

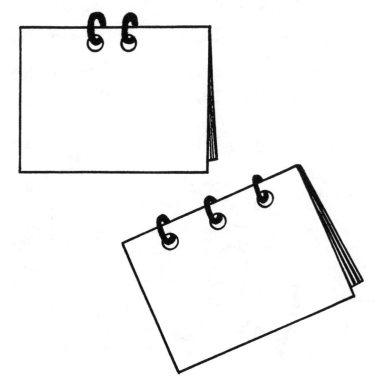

Laces. Punch two holes through the pages and covers. Use yarn, ribbon, string, shoestrings, or another type of cord to lace the book together.

Notebook Fasteners. Notebook fasteners come in varying lengths. Use whatever is available. Punch two holes through the pages and covers, placing the holes according to the size of fastener used. Notebook fasteners are a very sturdy type of binding.

Spiral Binding. Some schools have a machine for spiral binding.

Old Notebooks. The ring-strip or fastener-strip from old notebooks can be used as a binding method.

Fanfold Accordion Books

For fanfold books, tape together as many pages as are needed. If computer fanfold paper is used, tape along the fold line as reinforcement. Fanfold books also can be taped to open horizontally.

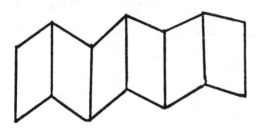

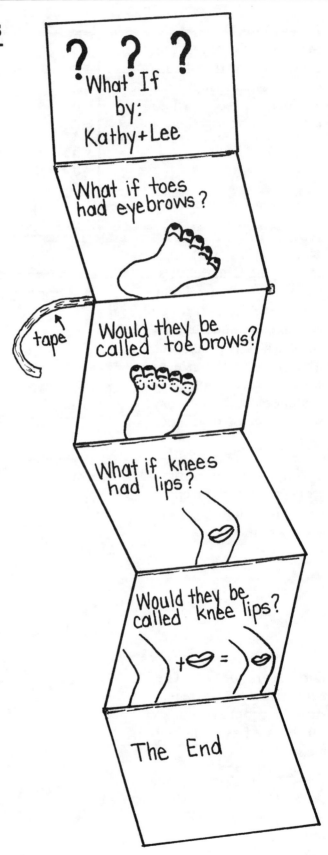

Binding Shape Books

Shape books can be assembled using the same techniques as regular books.

Staple and cover staples with tape

Lace with ribbon

Brass fasteners

Rings

Spiral binding

Notebook fasteners

Fanfold accordion pages

Cloth Binding: For That Favorite Book

1. Staple the pages of the book together.

2. Cut two pieces of cardboard slightly larger than the stapled pages. Lay the two pieces of cardboard out on a piece of cloth.

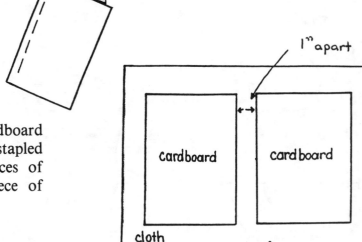

   Leave about an inch of space between the two pieces of cardboard.

   Trim the cloth so there is about a 2" cloth margin all the way around the cardboard pieces.

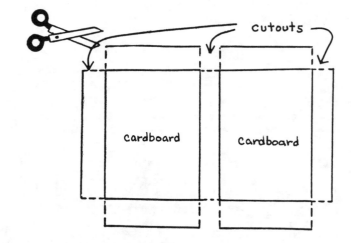

3. Cut out the cloth corners and slots at the middle between the cardboard.

4. Put the cardboard aside and paint glue on the cloth.

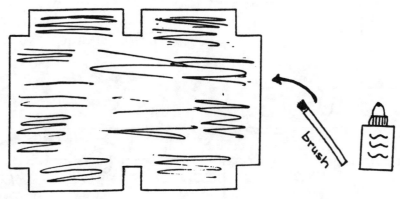

5. Place one piece of cardboard on the gluey cloth and fold the cloth over the edges of the cardboard.

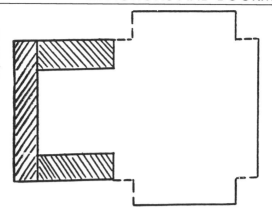

6. Do the same with the other piece of cardboard.

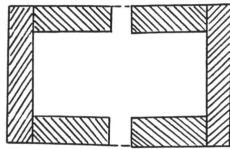

7. Place the stapled book pages along the gluey center strip.

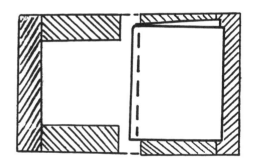

8. Close the cover. Staple along the edge through the cloth and the pages.

   To add a finished look, glue a piece of cloth over the cardboard on the inside front and back.

   Allow to dry. Decorate the cover.

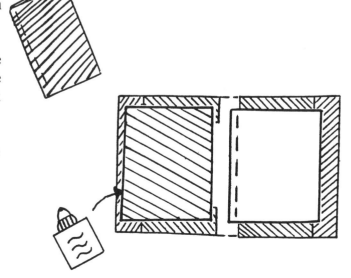

2 | Thematic Writing and Book Design

TEACHING WITH THEMATIC PROJECTS

How can lessons be facilitated so children not only learn but also are eager to continue learning? One way is to use bookmaking projects that focus on a particular theme, such as holidays or animals. Using thematic projects with lift-flap and pop-up books enhances classroom instruction and provides a valuable organizational tool for teachers who believe in the philosophy of integrated teaching.

Themes capture a child's imagination and interest because they provide learning experiences that have clear continuity. Themes offer exciting possibilities for integrating topics with specific children's books. Children's books are a starting point for inquiry and a resource for information.

Many thoughtful teachers see a need to complement the basic curriculum with small-group and individual activities. A good way to do this is to add project work to thematic study. Through an organized task directed toward a specific purpose, children are involved in the study of a topic over an extended period of time, ranging from several days to several weeks. Projects are usually done by children individually or in small groups of two to three children. Children begin with their own expressed interests or with suggestions offered by teachers. Bookmaking projects bring reading, writing, spelling, and listening together with the content areas of science, math, and social studies. Projects serve to clarify and extend ideas and give children a reason to apply their language arts skills in combination with content information. Using a book format for projects makes sense to children; they understand collecting information for reporting and sharing through books.

This section for teaching with projects is organized into themes, each with suggested projects for children to work on alone or collaboratively in producing their own lift-flap and pop-up books. Children should have some choice in what and how they learn. Allowing children choices in creating their own books can boost desire and spark lifelong interests. This section provides choices for thematic projects, choices that use literature as a springboard and encourage children to become involved in independent learning and doing.

Nearly every classroom lesson also provides open-ended opportunities. These are the times to continue with the topic and invite children to pursue bookmaking projects. The projects described in this section can be used as presented or adapted to personal situations to meet small-group and individual needs and interests.

TALES AND LEGENDS: FOLKLORE

Dearly loved by teachers and children, folk tales and legends express universal emotions: joy and sadness, contentment and fear, love and hate, generosity and jealousy. Tales and legends can enhance a curriculum with magic settings, victorious characters, and exciting plots. Old tales and legends may also lead to new writing opportunities: Pedro of *Pedro & the Padre* may continue his misadventures as he rides Panchita the burro, and Anansi the spider can be rescued again and again, all with the help of paper actions.

There's always enough stone soup to go around for everyone and enough mischief to be done to keep any number of Manx cats busy. A curriculum involving tales and legends is a curriculum of inspiration and aspiration.

Literature Springboard:

How the Manx Cat Lost Its Tail by Janet Stevens. New York: Harcourt Brace Jovanovich, 1990.

The ark is ready; Noah and his family and animals are ready. But where is the Manx cat? A humorous retelling of why Manx cats have no tails.

Project: Here, Kitty, Kitty

Objective: Students will record information about different kinds of cats.

Focus Question: What is unusual about a Manx cat?

Directions:

Locate the Isle of Man on a map and study pictures of Manx cats. Pique students' interest by talking about Siamese cats and Angora cats.

Work in pairs to find information about different kinds of cats, using trade and reference books. Prepare informational reports and add paper pop-ups for a book page. Assemble the pages into a book as a small-group project.

Criterion for Evaluation: Completed action book reporting information about different kinds of cats.

Sharing: Take the book to the local humane society and leave at the reception desk for others to read.

Another Springboard: *Old Noah's Elephant* by Warren Ludwig. New York: Putnam, 1991.

Literature Springboard:

You Bet Your Britches, Claude by Jean Lowery Nixon. New York: Puffin Books, 1989.
Shirley and Claude adopt Tom and then Bessie in a western tall-tale adventure.

Project: Western Conversation

Objective: Students will identify and write analogies.

Focus Question: How happy would you be if you were happier than a pig in a mud puddle?

Directions:

Talk about the following analogies from the book and how they help make comparisons:

- hot as the yolk of a just-fried egg

- waving her legs like a beetle on its back

- hopping like a frog on a hot rock

- the way a hungry rattlesnake smiles at a prairie dog

Work together in small groups to write what Claude, Shirley, Tom, and Bessie might say to describe objects and events, such as:

- the kindness of a neighbor

- the color of butter

- the price of long johns

- the bumpiness of a road

Give action to the pages with accordion folds, coils, or other movable features.

Criterion for Evaluation: Completed action page with analogies.

Sharing: Read the book to the principal.

Another Springboard: *Beats Me, Claude* by Joan Lowery Nixon. New York: Puffin Books, 1986.

Literature Springboard:

Pedro & the Padre by Verna Aardema. New York: Dial Books, 1991.

Pedro goes to seek his own fortune, plays tricks on those he meets, and finds himself in difficult predicaments.

Project: A Boy and a Burro

Objective: Students will apply creative writing and editing skills.

Focus Question: Suppose Panchita belonged to you. Where would you have her take you?

Directions:

Brainstorm other fortune-seeking adventures for Pedro and the faithful burro Panchita. Find imaginative ways for Pedro to solve difficulties along the way. Write the tale. Work in pairs or small groups to edit the first drafts. Use pull-tabs, slot-tabs, and pivot-tabs to move Pedro and Panchita. Assemble the pages for a book.

Criterion for Evaluation: Completed action book with creative Pedro and Panchita stories.

Sharing: Exchange books with other small groups.

Another Springboard: *It Could Always Be Worse* by Margot Zemach. New York: Farrar, Straus & Giroux, 1976.

Literature Springboard:

Anansi the Spider by Gerald McDermott. New York: Henry Holt and Company, 1987.

Anansi is threatened by terrible predicaments along his journey but is saved by his sons. Which son should be rewarded for saving Anansi?

Project: The Great Anansi Rescue

Objective: Students will pattern their own writing after the story structure of *Anansi the Spider*.

Focus Question: What are some other frightening times when Anansi might need to be rescued?

Directions:

Write another tale using a story pattern similar to the one in the book. Work in groups of six. Create six more sons or daughters for Anansi, each with his or her own unique ability. Invent six ways how each could rescue Anansi. Write a story, using your own names and the special abilities in the story. For example:

Where is Anansi now?
Anansi is in the oven.
Raymundo the Muscle Man will lift him out.
Where is Anansi now?
Anansi is falling from the airplane.
Adamaria the Flying Girl will catch him.

Assemble the story with paper actions.

Criterion for Evaluation: Completed action book using a patterned story structure.

Sharing: Read the book to any class that will recognize the personal names in the story.

Another Springboard: *The Ant and the Elephant* by Bill Peet. Boston: Houghton Mifflin, 1972.

Literature Springboard:

Turquoise Boy: A Navajo Legend by Terri Cohlene. Mahwah, NJ: Watermill Press, 1990.
    Turquoise Boy searches for a way to make life easier for his people, proves himself, and brings horses. Includes a helpful Navajo information appendix.

Project: Navajo Dictionary

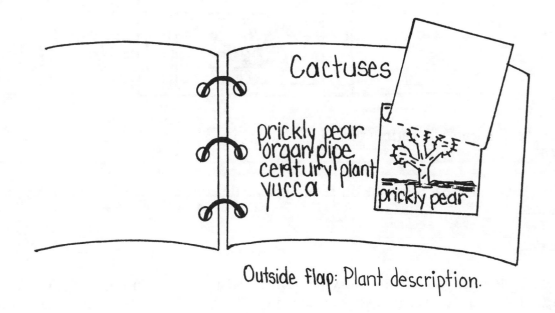

Outside flap: Plant description.

Objective: Students will increase their knowledge of Navajo vocabulary words.

Focus Question: What questions would you like to ask Turquoise Boy about the Navajo?

Directions:

Compile a dictionary of words and definitions related to the Navajo, such as Dinetaa, hogan, sand painting, mesa, and cactus. Place a selected word and a suitable paper action on each page.

Criterion for Evaluation: Completed book with accurate definitions and representations of the selected words.

Sharing: Read the book to a teacher in the school who has lived in or has a particular interest in the Southwest.

Another Springboard: *Dream Wolf* by Paul Goble. New York: Bradbury Press, 1990.

TURKEYS AND FIRECRACKERS: HOLIDAYS

Celebrating holidays is an important part of children's lives. Holidays are special times both to look forward to and to look back on. Every family ties many memories and traditions to holidays.

Watching fireworks explode over a field or over a bay can give rise to curiosity, such as when the first fireworks display began. And who hasn't wondered, at least fleetingly, what it was like at the very first Thanksgiving? And how did the giving of valentines on Valentine's Day start?

The curriculum at every grade recognizes the historical significance and fun surrounding holidays. Collecting information about holidays not only satisfies curiosity but also can result in holiday books to treasure, especially if the books have exploding firecracker paper movements or pop-up valentines for those people children care about.

Literature Springboard:

How Spider Saved Valentine's Day by Robert Kraus. New York: Scholastic, 1985.

Spider improvises a valentine for the two sleepy caterpillars, but before the valentine can be delivered two butterflies emerge.

Project: Time for a Party

Objective: Students will sequence job tasks for a valentine party.

Focus Question: Let's plan a valentine party. What do we need to do before the party, during the party, and after the party?

Directions:

On the chalkboard make three columns for the following job categories: jobs before the party; jobs during the party; and jobs after the party.

List as a class all the work that needs to be done to have a party. Working in pairs, sort each job into the category indicating when the job needs to be done. Come together as a class and make a master job chart; students then volunteer for all the jobs.

Working individually, make a lift-flap page of directions for carrying out a specific job. For example, "Clean up the room" might include:

1. Put all recyclable products in a bin.

2. Put dirty paper products in a garbage bag.

3. Put things to be washed near the sink.

4. Wash tables.

5. Sweep floor.

6. Put chairs back in order.

7. Turn out the lights. Assemble the pages as a party planner.

Have a valentine party!

Criterion for Evaluation: Completed pages for the party planner.

Sharing: Read to guests at the party.

Another Springboard: *Arthur's Valentine* by Marc Brown. Boston: Little, Brown, 1990.

Literature Springboard:

Fireworks, Picnics, and Flags by James Giblin. New York: Clarion Books, 1983.
Short historical stories of familiar national symbols are presented.

Project: Celebrating the Fourth of July

Objective: Students will learn the meaning behind national symbols.

Focus Questions: Is a bald eagle really bald? Who are the figures in the painting *The Spirit of '76*?

Directions:

Discuss topics such as the flag, fireworks, the eagle, the Liberty Bell, July picnics, and patriotic music. Select and research a Fourth of July topic using trade and reference books. Write a report about a national symbol and use an action page to demonstrate the information.

Criterion for Evaluation: Completed informational page with an action that demonstrates the focus of the report.

Sharing: Read the book to a war veteran. Give the book to a local veterans' hospital for the waiting room.

Another Springboard: *The Star-Spangled Banner* by Peter Spier. New York: Doubleday, 1973.

Literature Springboard:

The Little Old Lady Who Was Not Afraid of Anything by Linda Williams. New York: HarperTrophy, 1986.
    The little old lady goes walking in the woods and gets a noisy Halloween scare.

Project: Boo Book

Objective: Students will effectively use scary and spooky words.

Focus Question: How can we dress a scarecrow to be spooky and scary?

Directions:

Work in groups of five to make a Halloween page including:

- scary shoes (clomp, clomp)

- scary pants/skirt (wiggle, wiggle)

- scary gloves (clap, clap)

- scary pumpkin head (boo, boo)

Use V pop-ups (see pages 35-41) so the scary objects leap up and off the page. Include a list of Halloween words beside the movable objects. Save the last few pages for some assembled scarecrows that move up and down on a pivot.

Criterion for Evaluation: Completed boo book.

Sharing: Read the book to classmates.

Another Springboard: *It's Halloween* by Jack Prelutsky. New York: Greenwillow, 1977.

Literature Springboard:

It's Thanksgiving by Jack Prelutsky. New York: Scholastic, 1982.
   A set of 12 poems that are fun to read and reread.

Project: Thanksgiving Poem

Objective: Students will describe Thanksgiving events through poetry.

Focus Question: What are some of the things you like about Thanksgiving?

Directions:

   Brainstorm Thanksgiving topics and sets of rhyming words. Create a poem. Illustrate the poem using fold-a-frames. Assemble all the poems as a class book.

Criterion for Evaluation: Completed poetry action book.

Sharing: Read aloud the day before Thanksgiving while enjoying traditional foods.

Another Springboard: *Silly Tilly's Thanksgiving* by Lillian Hoban. New York: Harper-Trophy, 1990.

Literature Springboard:

Let's Celebrate! by Peter Roop and Connie Roop. Minneapolis, MN: Lerner, 1986.
   Riddles about the holidays bring a giggle.

Project: Playing with Words

Objective: Students will extend their enjoyment of holidays through humor.

Focus Question: How can you amuse family members at a holiday get-together?

Directions:

   Select a holiday and write a holiday riddle page using lift-flaps. Assemble the lift-flap pages for a class book. Holiday riddles may read "Why is turkey a good holiday food? Because you can gobble it up."

Criterion for Evaluation: Completed riddle book using lift-flap surprises.

Sharing: Read the riddles to the student safety patrols.

Another Springboard: *Arthur's April Fool* by Marc Brown. Boston: Little, Brown, 1983.

YOU AND ME: FAMILY AND FRIENDS

Family is the basis for every child's day, and friends bring the rich enjoyment that enhances life. Family and friends give children a sense of connection and the security to try out new adventures.

The school curriculum includes units on family life, respecting others, and self-esteem. Reading about other people, other families, and other relationships helps students recognize the diversity associated with today's families. Yet, there are universal situations of helping each other, taking turns, and having fun.

Writing books about family and friends gives children a chance to personally profile their lives and to express their joy, curiosity, and creativity. Paper actions add the extra fun.

Literature Springboard:

Never Spit on Your Shoes by Denys Cazet. New York: Orchard Books, 1990.

A first-grader tells his mother about his first day of school while the illustrations tell the "real" story.

Project: What Happened Next?

Objective: Students will sequence the events of a school day.

Focus Question: Have you ever tried to brush your teeth before you put the toothpaste on the toothbrush?

Directions:

   Review sequencing as the order in which things happen. Talk about signal words such as *next, then, after that,* and *finally*.
   Write one page each about events during your day. Illustrate each entry using turn wheels or pull-tabs. Working in groups of five, sequence the pages as the events happened during the day.

Criterion for Evaluation: Completed action book showing sequenced events.

Sharing: Take your book home and read it to your parents. Students also can create a book about their parent's day.

Another Springboard: *Alexander and the Terrible, Horrible, No Good, Very Bad Day* by Judith Viorst. New York: Atheneum, 1972.

Literature Springboard:

Birthday Present by Cynthia Rylant. New York: Orchard Books, 1987.
   The joy of getting a year older and having birthday celebrations is something special to remember. A big celebration for every birthday is a must.

Project: Happy Birthday!

Objective: Students will explore birthday gift options.

Focus Question: What can you give a friend for his or her birthday that doesn't cost money?

Directions:

Have students discuss how both the giver and the receiver feel about a hug, help washing the car, and help sweeping the sidewalk. Discuss how much money the things on the list cost.

Work individually to make your own birthday gift list. The next time someone you know has a birthday, what could you give him or her that is special but doesn't cost money? Present the gifts by making a lift-flap book of birthday coupons such as, "This coupon is worth one hug," "This coupon is good to have the trash taken out once," and others. Under the coupon lift-flap is a picture of the gift. Assemble your coupons as an individual book.

Criterion for Evaluation: Completed coupon lift-flap book showing the gifts.

Sharing: Read your book to a friend and display at the school store.

Another Springboard: *Handtalk Birthday: A Number and Story Book in Sign Language* by Remy Charlip, Mary Beth Miller, and George Ancona. New York: Four Winds, 1987.

Literature Springboard:

Picnic by Emily McCully. New York: Harper & Row, 1984.

A family of mice lose one of their children on the way to a picnic. All ends well in this wordless picture book when the lost mouse child is found.

Project: Where Are You?

Objective: Students will create further adventures for a tale.

Focus Question: How would it feel to be lost?

Directions:

Discuss being lost. What would you do? Evaluate whether the mouse in the story did the right thing. Brainstorm further adventures for the mouse. Work in pairs to write a tale. Have another pair edit the work. Use pull-tabs, pivot-tabs, or other actions to move scenes for the book. Assemble the pages for a book.

Criterion for Evaluation: Completed action book of the mouse's adventures.

Sharing: Read to the school media specialist and display in the media center.

Another Springboard: *Mr. Grumpy's Outing* by John Burningham. New York: Holt, Rinehart & Winston, 1970.

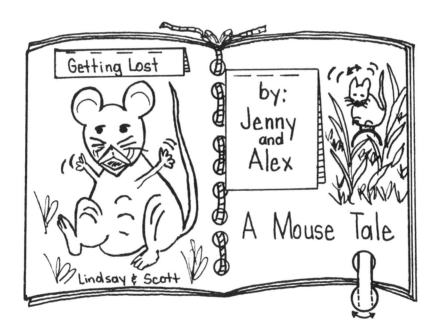

Literature Springboard:

The Computer Rules by Alvin Granowsky, Joy Ann Tweedt, and Craig Tweedt. Cleveland, OH: Modern Curriculum Press, 1985.
A family discovers that they need rules for using their new home computer.

Project: It's My Turn!

Objective: Students will record rules for using a shared item in the home.

Focus Question: Do you ever argue over whose turn it is to do something?

Directions:

Discuss why classroom rules are important. Discuss how family rules are important to avoid arguments. Role-play what would happen if there were no rules in the classroom. Individually, write rules for using a shared item in your home. Make a turn wheel to show the rules. Assemble all the different rule pages as a class book.

Criterion for Evaluation: Completed action book of rules.

Sharing: Display on the appropriate appliance at home.

Another Springboard: *How to Talk to Your Computer* by Seymour Simon. New York: Thomas Y. Crowell, 1985.

Literature Springboard:

The Purple Door by Janifer De Vos. Portland, OR: Multnomah, 1990.
    Erin has an adventure behind the purple door that tests her loyalty and endurance. Part I of the Guardian Series.

Project: Behind the Door

Objective: Students will make logical predictions.

Focus Questions: If you happened upon a locked door, would you want to find out what was behind it? Why?

Directions:

Brainstorm what could be behind a locked door. Discuss how reasoning skills help in all professions. Write a family tale. Display the first part of the tale on the outside of the door and the ending under the door lift-flap. Readers predict the ending.

Criterion for Evaluation: Completed page for a class lift-flap book.

Sharing: Read the book to your family. Ask them to predict endings to the tales.

Another Springboard: *Who's in Rabbit's House?* by Verna Aardema. New York: Dial, 1977.

LIVING AND BREATHING: ANIMALS

Animals are among children's first loves. From their first teddy bear to fantasy characters to fact-filled books of animal lore, animals occupy a large part of students' reading. Animals can be a child's introduction to the field of science.

Slippery eels, slithering snakes, porky pigs, and enormous elephants all can come alive through the fun of movable paper actions. Birds fly on the pages and salmon swim upstream. Paper actions can give animals, real or imagined, dimensions of running, leaping, or even sleeping. Touching, holding, and caring about real or imagined animals helps children become involved, empathetic readers, and movable paper actions can add to that involvement.

Literature Springboard:

A Chick Hatches by Joanna Cole. New York: Morrow, 1976.
    The development of a chick from egg to hatching.

Project: Eggs and Chicks

Objective: Students will develop vocabulary to write about egg reproduction.

Focus Question: What does incubation mean?

Directions:

List vocabulary words needed to write about reproduction, such as *egg, fertilize, incubate*, and *hatch*. Write the steps to describe the process of egg to chick, and use accordion books to show the progression.

Criterion for Evaluation: Completed accordion book.

Sharing: Read the book to the school nurse and display in the school clinic.

Another Springboard: *Inside an Egg* by Sylvia Johnson. Minneapolis, MN: Lerner Publications, 1982.

Literature Springboard:

Snake by Michael Chinery. Mahwah, NJ: Troll Associates, 1991.

An introduction to the characteristics and environment of snakes.

Project: Slippery, Slithering Snakes

Objective: Students will understand snakes as part of the balance of nature.

Focus Question: Despite their bad reputation, snakes have good qualities. What good things do you know about snakes?

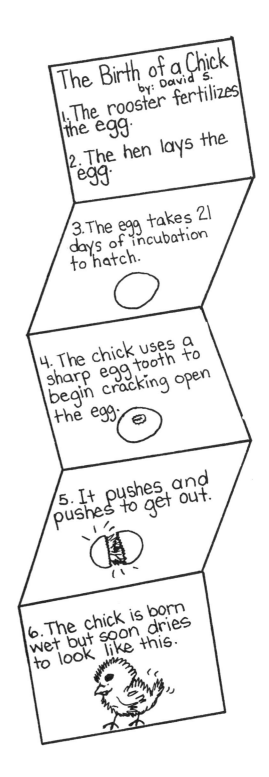

Directions:

Discuss snakes and misconceptions about snakes. Work in pairs to write a factual paragraph about snakes. Use coils or springs to make an action page to go with the paragraph. Assemble the pages as a class book.

Criterion for Evaluation: Completed action book about snakes.

Sharing: Read the book to someone who has a pet snake. Display the book in a science center.

Another Springboard: *Earthworms* by Terry Jennings. New York: Gloucester Press, 1990.

Literature Springboard:

Bugs by Nancy Parker and Joan Wright. New York: Mulberry Books, 1987.
    Includes information, descriptions, and jokes about a variety of common insects.

Project: Ugh! Bugs!

Objective: Students will extend their description skills.

Focus Question: Does a slug have the same characteristics as an insect?

Directions:

Select an insect to describe. Write the description as a riddle. Answer the riddle using a paper action in the shape of a talking mouth.

It can hop
on a dog. It
could make
him sick.

by: Chelsea

Answer can be in the tick's mouth or under a flap.

Criterion for Evaluation: Completed book with a talking mouth.

Sharing: Read to a teacher who has spiders or butterflies in the classroom. Display in that teacher's classroom.

Another Springboard: *The Hidden World: Life Under a Rock* by Laurence Pringle. New York: Macmillan, 1977.

Literature Springboard:

Animals Should Definitely Not Act Like People by Judi Barrett. New York: Macmillan, 1980.

Cleverly illustrated pictures show how inconvenient it would be if animals behaved like people.

Project: Alliterating Animals

Objective: Students will use alliteration to write tongue twisters.

Focus Question: Do dainty dogs dance dangerously?

Directions:

Discuss alliteration. Talk about the adjective, noun, verb, adverb sentence pattern.
Work in pairs. Select a letter of the alphabet and an animal starting with that letter. Write a sentence tongue twister with all words beginning with the selected letter of the alphabet. Use paper actions to give more fun to your tongue twister. Assemble all the tongue twisters as a class book.

Criteria for Evaluation: Completed alliteration action pages.

Sharing: Have a contest to see who can read each tongue twister the fastest.

Another Springboard: *One Fish, Two Fish, Red Fish, Blue Fish* by Dr. Seuss. New York: Random House, 1960.

Literature Springboard:

Louis the Fish by Arthur Yorinks. New York: Farrar, Straus & Giroux, 1980.
    Louis is transformed from a butcher who hates meat into his fantasy, a fish.

Project: A Fish Story

Objective: Students will sequence events in a life story.

Focus Question: Have you ever wished to be something or somebody else?

Directions:

    List the events in Louis's life. Put the events in the order in which they happened. Make an action page to accompany each event. Assemble the page sequences to make a book.

Criterion for Evaluation: Completed sequence action book.

Sharing: Read the book to a teacher who likes to go fishing. Display in the teacher's room that has an aquarium.

Another Springboard: *The Story of Chicken Licken* by Jan Ormerod. New York: Lothrop, Lee & Shepard, 1985.

RIDDLES AND RHYMES: WORD FUN

Jokes and riddles beg to be shared orally. There is a happy interaction of, "Listen to this one!" "Knock, knock" is sure to bring a quick response of "Who's there?" with fun word sounds to follow. Active involvement includes memorizing "the really good ones." Riddles are fun to read and just as much fun to write.

Rhyming lines in books give children joyous language experiences. The rhyming often leads to predictable words for group participation. The rhyming patterns provide a story structure that serves as a model for independent writing. Rhymes need an audience. Pop-up actions add something special to involve the audience.

Literature Springboard:

In the Doghouse! by Sharon Friedman and Irene Shere. Minneapolis, MN: Lerner Publications, 1986.
The jokes about dogs are amusing for young as well as older children.

Project: Jokers and Aces

Objective: Students will smile, giggle, and laugh out loud.

Focus Questions: Have you ever looked at a dog and thought that it was smiling? Do dogs smile? If so, what do you think they smile about?

Directions:

Select an animal. Make up riddles about the animal, such as "What did the dog take along on a camping trip? A pup tent!" Use playing-card shapes for the book pages that contain the riddles. Include a joker. Use lift-flaps to help tell the riddles.

Under flap: Spring!

Criterion for Evaluation: Completed lift-flap riddle pages.

Sharing: Read the riddles to your classmates. Display your book in the office for visitors to enjoy.

Another Springboard: *Going Buggy* by Peter Roop and Connie Roop. Minneapolis, MN: Lerner Publications, 1986.

Literature Springboard:

Sheep in a Jeep by Nancy Shaw. Boston: Houghton Mifflin, 1986.
   The sheep are not adept at driving a jeep, and hilarious rhyming adventures result.

Project: Rhymes and Stories

Objective: Students will develop skill in using rhyming words to convey a story.

Focus Question: What are your favorite *Sheep in a Jeep* words?

Directions:

Select an animal and a vehicle. Work in pairs or in a small group. Brainstorm the story content. Write a page, such as:

- Frogs on a bike

- Frogs steer

- Frogs veer

- Frogs smash

- Frogs in the trash

Set each page to a paper action. Assemble the pages for a group or class book.

Criterion for Evaluation: Completed rhyme book with action pages.

Sharing: Put two or three books in a bookbag for an overnight check-out. Read the books to parents.

Another Springboard: *The Owl and the Pussycat* by Edward Lear. Illustrated by Jan Brett. New York: Putnam, 1991.

Literature Springboard:

Is Your Mama a Llama? by Deborah Guarino. New York: Scholastic, 1989.

Lloyd the llama asks in rhyme whether the other baby animals have a llama mama. Lynn the llama gives the right answer. Steven Kellogg's illustrations add pleasure to the rhyming text.

Project: Lloyd the Llama Goes Snorkeling

Objective: Students will develop the skill of describing things.

Focus Question: Is your mama a llama?

Directions:

Lloyd goes snorkeling one day and continues to ask the underwater creatures whether their mama is a llama. Select an underwater creature to describe. Write a reply to Lloyd's question and use a talking mouth. Combine the pages to make an action book.

Criterion for Evaluation: Completed water-world action book.

Sharing: Read the book to all the classes that have fish tanks.

Another Springboard: *A Mouse in My House* by Nancy Van Laan. New York: Knopf, 1990.

Literature Springboard:

A Teacher on Roller Skates by David Adler. New York: Holiday House, 1989.

This riddle collection about school and teachers has black-and-white line illustrations that encourage students to try their own drawings.

Project: Riddles

Objective: Students will enjoy word plays for riddles.

Focus Question: How does humor make work more enjoyable?

Directions:

Working in pairs, select an occupation. Write riddles using the occupation as a unifying theme. Make a lift-flap page for each riddle. Assemble the pages as a small-group book.

Criterion for Evaluation: Completed lift-flap riddle book.

Sharing: Read to friends and neighbors in the chosen occupation.

Another Springboard: *Riddle Roundup* by Giulio Maestro. New York: Clarion, 1989.

Literature Springboard:

Put Me in the Zoo by Robert Lopshire. New York: Random House, 1988.

Easy to memorize, fast-paced rhyming lines are fun to read for every age.

Project: Binoculars

Objective: Students will use rhymes to express their ideas.

Focus Question: If you had a hundred spots in your pocket, what would you do with them?

Directions:

Talk about the fun sounds of rhyming words. Select an animal. Write about the neat things that the animal can do. Write your ideas in rhyme and use lift-flaps to reveal what the animal can do. Assemble your pages as a rhyming book.

Criterion for Evaluation: Completed action-filled rhyming book.

Sharing: Read your book on an audiotape. Share the book and the tape with the kindergarten.

Another Springboard: *Hop on Pop* by Dr. Seuss. New York: Random House, 1963.

PROFILES AND PATRIOTS: BIOGRAPHIES

Some leaders had a presidential future and some were destined to command armies. Some would have an aviation future and some would lead slaves to freedom. Some leaders were friendly or solitary, and others were courageous or afraid. Each contributed in his or her own way.

The public and private lives of U.S. leaders give glimpses into historical times and events. Deeds stand alone and let us know the strength of convictions and commitment. Biographies share human details, exciting feats, and the little incidents that make a person's life interesting.

Biographies bring to a curriculum the standards of a person's life, the ideals to reach for, and an understanding of human fallibility. Paper actions can re-create history.

Literature Springboard:

George Washington's Breakfast by Jean Fritz. New York: Coward-McCann, 1969.

George Washington Allen learns about a breakfast of the past and gets his grandmother to cook it.

Project: Recipes

Objective: Students will write measurements for breakfast.

Focus Questions: How is your breakfast different from George Washington's? How is it the same?

Directions:

Bring from home a favorite family recipe. Study the ingredient measurements. Write a recipe using one-half, one-third, or one-quarter the amounts. Use turn wheels to put the ingredients together for a meal. Assemble the recipe pages for a book.

Criterion for Evaluation: Completed recipe turn-wheel book.

Sharing: Read the book to the cafeteria workers. Display by the cafeteria cashier.

Another Springboard: *And Then What Happened Paul Revere?* by Jean Fritz. New York: Coward-McCann, 1973.

Literature Springboard:

Amelia Earhart by Richard Tames. New York: Franklin Watts, 1989.
    A carefully researched biography of Earhart.

Project: Flying

Objective: Students will seek information from reference books.

Focus Question: One of the first ways to learn about flying is to fly a kite. Why does a kite fly?

Directions:

Read about kites. Record information about kites that really interests you. Make a book page reporting about a kite. Name the kite and add movements. Assemble all the pages for a kite book.

Criterion for Evaluation: Completed kite book with paper actions.

Sharing: Read the book to parents and other visitors at the school or class science fair.

Another Springboard: *Sally Ride and the New Astronauts* by Karen O'Connor. New York: Franklin Watts, 1983.

Literature Springboard:

Wanted Dead or Alive: The True Story of Harriet Tubman by Ann McGovern. New York: Scholastic, 1965.
   The story of how Harriet Tubman led slaves to freedom through the Underground Railroad.

Project: Freedom

Objective: Students will record a sequence of biographical events.

Focus Question: What does it mean to admire someone?

Directions:

List on strips of paper various events in Harriet's life. Arrange the events in the order in which they happened. Select an event that you find interesting and describe that event. Work in pairs to make an action picture to accompany the event. Assemble the pages for a book.

Criteria for Evaluation: Completed biographical sequential action pages.

Sharing: Make a video for Black History Month.

Another Springboard: *Martin Luther King* by Rae Bains. Mahwah, NJ: Troll Associates, 1985.

Literature Springboard:

Robert E. Lee by Carol Greene. Chicago: Children's Press, 1989.
Black-and-white photographs add historical accuracy to this easy to read biography of Lee.

Project: Lee's Accomplishments

Objective: Students will develop a definition for an accomplishment.

Focus Question: Pretend you lived with Robert E. Lee. What would your life be like?

Directions:

Brainstorm a list of the accomplishments of General Lee. Use lift-flaps to pictorially show the accomplishments. Select a timeline of years and arrange the lift-flap pages in a biographical sequence to assemble a book.

Criteria for Evaluation: Completed lift-flap scenes of Lee's accomplishments.

Sharing: Read the book to a teacher who is very interested in history.

Another Springboard: *Molly Pitcher* by Jan Gleter and Kathleen Thompson. Nashville, TN: Ideals Publishing, 1985.

Literature Springboard:

Book of Black Heroes from A to Z by Wade Hudson and Valerie Wesley. Orange, NJ: Just Us Books, 1988.

An alphabet book of black men and women who have overcome obstacles to make significant contributions.

Project: Peary and Henson

Objective: Students will explore the North Pole through reading.

Focus Question: What does an explorer do?

Directions:

Find out what the weather is like at the North Pole. Read reference books about Matthew Henson. Plan to go to the North Pole with Robert Peary and Matthew Henson. Describe the trip through writing and paper actions. Assemble the information and actions for a book.

Criterion for Evaluation: Completed polar exploration book with paper actions.

Sharing: Read to a teacher who has lived in a very cold climate.

Another Springboard: Jackie Robinson by Carol Greene. Chicago: Children's Press, 1990.

ASK AND WONDER: OUR EARTH

Our Earth is amazing, and reading about it can be lots of fun. Through books, children can enter a world where swamps walk and frozen soil can produce trees. Children can read about seas of sand and meat-eating plants, about living coral and a river of grass. Our planet makes us ask questions and wonder about the answers.

Action books can enhance that wonder. Lightning can flash, raindrops can fall, and volcanoes can erupt, all through movable paper actions. These activities can add to the fun of enjoying earth science in a way that delights both students and teachers. The more children know about the planet, the more they will be willing to protect its environment.

Literature Springboard:

Raindrops and Rainbows by Rose Wyler. New York: Julian Messner, 1989.

Shows how and why it rains through demonstrations of simple experiments.

Project: The Weather

Objective: Students will feel the weather through poetry.

Focus Question: How does a rainy day make you feel?

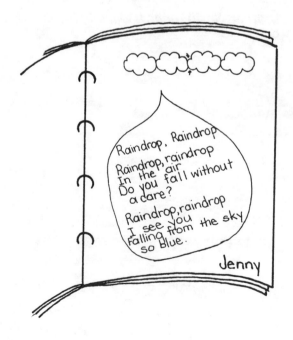

Directions:

Discuss words associated with rain. Group the rhyming words together. Discuss other weather conditions and list rhyming words. Create a poem showing a rainy day mood or other weather mood. Use accordion folds to stretch clouds or rainbows across the page of poetry. Assemble a class poetry book.

Criterion for Evaluation: Completed poem book with paper actions.

Sharing: Save the book for a rainy or snowy day and then read to each other.

Another Springboard: *Rainbows Are Made* by Lee Bennett Hopkins. San Diego: Harcourt Brace Jovanovich, 1982.

Literature Springboard:

Quicksand and Other Earthly Wonders by Q. L. Pearce. Englewood Cliffs, NJ: Julian Messner, 1989.

Amazing facts and features of our planet are presented. The information helps to interest children in earth science.

Project: Earth Facts

Objective: Students will seek information about our amazing Earth.

Focus Question: How many ants live in an ant hill?

Directions:

Discuss our Earth wonders: canyons, mountains, rivers, swamps. Locate on a map various Earth wonders. Write a report about a particular wonder that has high interest to you, such as the Florida Everglades. Use a paper action to give movement to your Earth wonder. Assemble an Earth wonder book.

Criterion for Evaluation: Completed action book about Earth wonders.

Sharing: Read the book to the worker who comes to trim the bushes and mow the grass in the schoolyard. Display in a science center.

Another Springboard: *The Living World* by Tony Seddon and Jill Baily. Garden City, NY: Doubleday, 1986.

Literature Springboard:

Growing Vegetable Soup by Lois Ehlert. San Diego: Harcourt Brace Jovanovich, 1987.
   The vegetables are planted, harvested, and then made into soup.

Project: Alphabet Soup

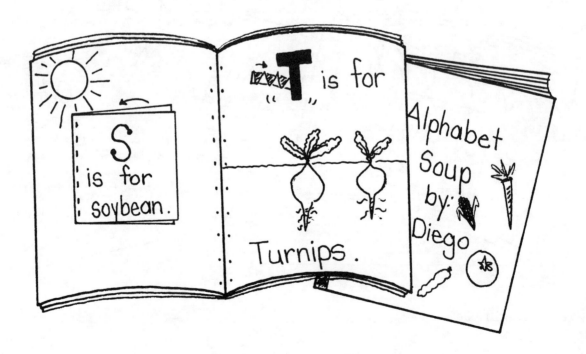

Objective: Students will identify different vegetables.

Focus Question: Is a leek good to eat?

Directions:

Use trade and reference books to collect the names of vegetables eaten in the United States and other countries. Make a vegetable A-B-C book. Use folded springs so the letter of the alphabet pops up from the page. Write information about each vegetable. At the end of the book, mix up the vegetables to make alphabet soup.

Criterion for Evaluation: Completed alphabet action book.

Sharing: Invite parents in to help make alphabet soup. Read the book together while enjoying the soup.

Another Springboard: The Scoop on Ice Cream by Vicki Cobb. Boston: Little, Brown, 1985.

Literature Springboard:

El Libro de las Estaciones (A Book of Seasons) by Alice Provensen and Martin Provensen. New York: Random House, 1982.

A book of the changing seasons presented in Spanish and English.

Project: Through the Year

Objective: Students will compare and contrast the seasons.

Focus Question: Is it cold in December in every part of the world?

Directions:

Discuss what "the changing seasons" means. Select a season or month. Find out what that season is like in different parts of the world. Use paper actions to show similarities and differences of the season. Assemble four books, one for each season.

Criterion for Evaluation: Completed action book with accurate information.

Sharing: Read to the school secretary and place in the office next to the school calendar.

Another Springboard: *Anno's Journey* by Mitsumasa Anno. New York: Philomel, 1977.

Literature Springboard:

Sun Up, Sun Down by Gail Gibbons. San Diego: Harcourt Brace Jovanovich, 1983.
   Explains how life on Earth is regulated by the sun.

Project: The Sun

Objective: Students will extend their knowledge about the sun.

Focus Question: What would happen if there were no sun for a year?

Directions:

Darken the classroom and experience life "in the dark." Brainstorm what we know about the sun. Study the phenomenon of an eclipse. Describe the events of an eclipse. Discuss how early humans must have been mystified by an eclipse. Make an action book about an eclipse, using pull-tabs to hide the sun.

Criterion for Evaluation: Completed pull-tab book.

Sharing: Take home overnight and read to parents.

Another Springboard: *In a Dark, Dark Wood* selected by June Melsu and Joy Crowley. Bothell, WA: Wright Story Box Group, 1980.

WHEELS AND WINGS: TRANSPORTATION

The wheel is probably the most important invention ever made. The first wheels were sections cut through logs that were crude but effective. Size and style of wheels may have changed over time, but the shape hasn't. Wheels have given us cars, trains, airplanes, wagons, and bicycles—ways to travel from place to place, to transport things quickly and conveniently, and to fulfill our dreams and ambitions.

The possibilities for using wheels and wings to interest students in reading and writing about transportation are really limitless. One good book serves as an activity starter, and then there is a flourishing of both teacher and student ideas. Paper actions for wheels and wings can help students understand the development of the bicycle or interest students in knowing more about police cars. Wheels and wings give the curriculum a passage through time, bringing alive the past and the future.

Literature Springboard:

Cars by Angela Royston. New York: Macmillan, 1991.

Detailed pictures of young children's favorite cars are shown with features presented as inset enlargements for easy study.

Project: Victory Lane

Objective: Students will expand their technical vocabulary by labeling working parts of the car.

Focus Question: What is the difference between an accessory and a basic car part?

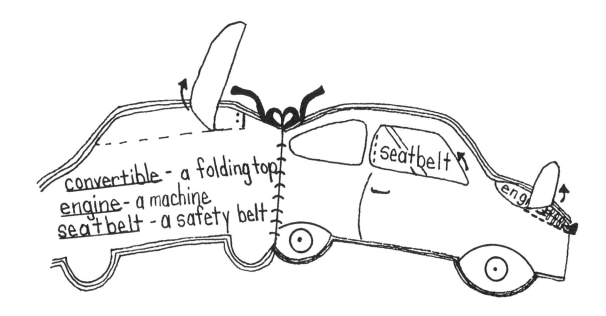

Directions:

Race to the victory lane by reviewing vocabulary words. Define and illustrate parts of a car using lift-flaps. Include such words as convertible, engine, and seatbelt. Use as a personal spelling challenge. Also include words with many meanings, such as *hood, exhaust*, and *spare*.

Criterion for Evaluation: Completed action book with accurate placement of the lift-flap car parts.

Sharing: Invite a parent who works on cars to stop by the classroom, perhaps when he or she is test driving a car or picking up parts. Read the book to the mechanic.

Another Springboard: *Monster Movers* by George Ancona. New York: Dutton, 1983.

Literature Springboard:

Wheels by Venice Shone. New York: Scholastic, 1990.
Emergency wheels, working wheels, vacation wheels, and others are pictured with accessories.

Project: Police Cars

Objective: Students will develop positive attitudes toward community workers by exploring the kind of work they do.

Focus Question: How do automobiles help police workers?

Directions:

Police work helps every community. Plan to have an officer come to the school's parking lot in a police car. Prepare for the visit by developing interview questions about police work and how the police car helps with that work. Ask the interview questions when the officer comes. Ask the officer to point out various features of the police car. Summarize your findings in an exciting V pop-up book. Use one page to describe and show each feature.

Criterion for Evaluation: Completed pop-up book with police car features and how these features help an officer.

Sharing: Have the officer stop by very briefly for a second time and read the book to him or her.

Another Springboard: *School Bus* by Donald Crews. New York: Greenwillow, 1984.

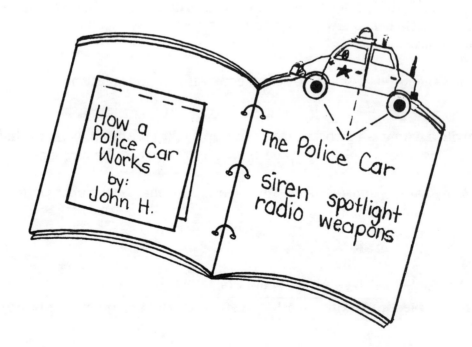

Literature Springboard:

Bikes by Anne Rockwell. New York: Dutton Children's Books, 1987.

Animal children ride unicycles, tandems, racing bikes, trail bikes, and exercise bikes.

Project: Bikes for Everyone

Objective: Students will apply research skills by recording a history of the bicycle.

Focus Question: What did early bicycles look like?

Directions:

A history of the bicycle moves from the 1790s to the present. Write a historical account of the bicycle. Use timelines and reference books. Include today's bicycles, such as dirt BMX bikes, folding bikes, tandems, and bikes for the handicapped. Give action to the history with pull-tabs.

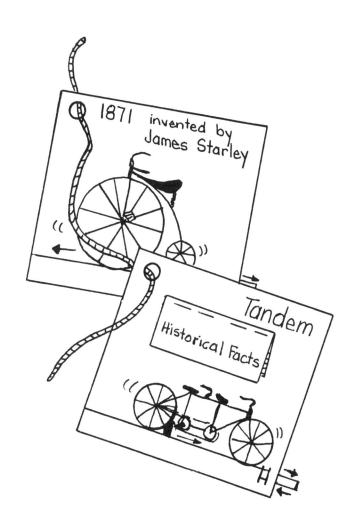

Criterion for Evaluation: Completed pull-tab book depicting the development of the bicycle.

Sharing: Read the book to a teacher in the school who bicycles as a hobby. Display the book in the library.

Another Springboard: Bicycles Are Fun to Ride by Dorothy Chlad. Chicago: Children's Press, 1984.

Literature Springboard:

On Wheels! by Phillippa Algeo. Milwaukee, WI: Gareth Stevens Publishing, 1986.

Wheeled vehicles are shown from a historical, then-and-now perspective.

Project: The Wagon Caravan

Objective: Students will contemplate the possibilities of what life was like in the past.

Focus Question: What will you load in your covered wagon before you start for the West?

Directions:

Covered wagons carried all the provisions pioneers needed for the long trek west. Load a covered wagon with "essentials." Use trade and reference books to get information to help you decide what to take. Use a lift-flap to reveal what is loaded in each wagon. Put all together, the wagons become a caravan book.

Criterion for Evaluation: Completed action book with each wagon loaded with essentials for traveling west in 1849.

Sharing: Read to small groups of students who will be studying the Western Movement next year.

Another Springboard: *The Josefina Story Quilt* by Eleanor Coerr. New York: Harper-Trophy, 1986.

Literature Springboard:

Tell Me About Wings, Wheels and Sails by Tom Stacy. New York: Random House, 1990.
　　Different forms of transportation are presented through a question-and-answer format.

Project: In the Air

Objective: The students will acquire new vocabulary words by exploring what it is like to fly in the air in a hot air balloon.

Focus Question: How are a hot air balloon and the Goodyear blimp the same?

Directions:

A is for air, B is for basket, and C is for chute. Use words unique to the world of ballooning to make an alphabet book. Use fold-a-frame pages to sequence the alphabet. Add factual information to the page about each alphabet item.

Criterion for Evaluation: For each student, a completed segment of the alphabet book that includes accurate definitions.

Sharing: Read the book to other classes and display as a book report.

Another Springboard: *The Twenty-One Balloons* by William P. du Bois. New York: Puffin Books, 1986.

T-SHIRTS AND SWEAT SOCKS: SPORTS

Sports are enjoyed by almost all children. Sports fill many leisure hours for all ages. Toddlers happily toss and kick a ball in any direction, and young adults dream of professional sports or of winning the Olympic gold medal. Sport stories often are motivational. Reluctant readers will immerse themselves in exciting sports stories even though they profess an unwillingness to read.

Paper movements can bring action to a sporting event. Watch the baseball streak out of the stadium! See how high the hot air balloon can soar in the race! A turn wheel can present the rules for playing soccer in an easy-to-review format. Movable books involve children in the excitement of a sports story.

Literature Springboard:

The Big Balloon Race by Eleanor Coerr. New York: Harper & Row, 1981.
    The day of the big race, Ariel helps her mother win a hot air balloon race.

Project: Up and Away

Objective: Students will make scientific predictions about heat and volume.

Focus Question: What does a hot air balloonist do if suddenly a tall object appears directly in front of the balloon?

Directions:

Discuss the importance of keeping calm in potentially dangerous hot air balloon situations. Discuss options for handling each situation.

Research hot air balloons and how they operate. Decide on the best option in a dangerous hot air balloon situation and show that option through a lift-flap. Assemble the situation pages for a class book.

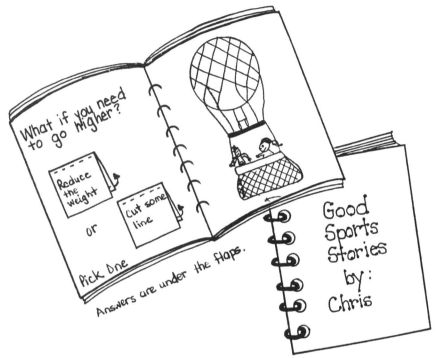

Criterion for Evaluation: Completed lift-flap book.

Sharing: Read the book to a teacher who has a keen interest in science.

Another Springboard: *The Glorious Flight* by Alice Provensen and Martin Provensen. New York: Puffin Books, 1983.

Literature Springboard:

The Berenstain Bears: Ready, Get Set, Go! by Stan Berenstain and Jan Berenstain. New York: Random House, 1988.

The bears compete in sports events while demonstrating the comparison of adjectives.

Project: Good, Better, Best

Objective: Students will use research skills to record a history of the Olympic Games.

Focus Question: What facts about the first Olympic Games can you share with us?

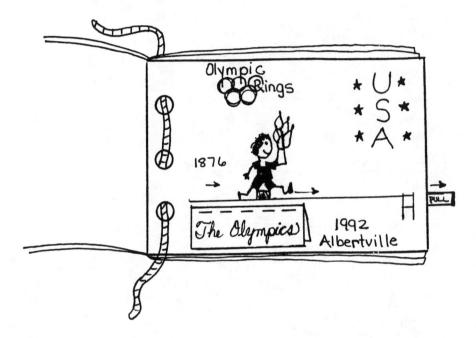

Directions:

Find pictures of Olympic medalists and events. Work in groups of three to research the Olympic flag, the first Olympics, a timeline of the Olympic years, the origin of the Olympics, and Greece and the Olympics. Use pull-tabs to show important Olympic milestone events.

Criterion for Evaluation: Completed pull-tab action book.

Sharing: Read the book to a school sports team.

Another Springboard: *Mary Lou Retton* by George Sullivan. New York: Julian Messner, 1985.

Literature Springboard:

Jackie Robinson and the Story of All-Black Baseball by Jim O'Connor. New York: Random House, 1989.
   A story of the first black major league baseball player and a history of all-black baseball teams.

Project: Baseball Diamond

Objective: Students will extend their map-making skills.

Focus Question: There are nine players on a baseball team. Each player has a position on the field. What are the nine positions called?

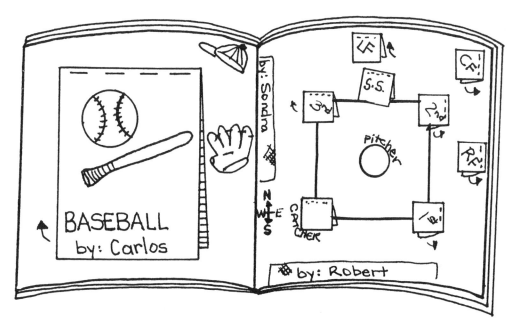

Names of players are under the flaps.

Directions:

Read more about Jackie Robinson and his accomplishments. Determine what position on the team Jackie played. Discuss the positions and the importance of each for a team. Make a map depicting the baseball positions. Use lift-flaps and list underneath baseball greats who have played the positions.

Criterion for Evaluation: Completed lift-flap book.

Sharing: Read the book to the physical education coach. Display in the coach's office.

Another Springboard: *The Year of the Boar and Jackie Robinson* by Betty Bao Lord. New York: Harper & Row, 1984.

Literature Springboard:

Major-League Melissa by Gibbs Davis. New York: Bantam Skylark, 1991.

Melissa, the team's star player, is upset when her horse collection is missing. Friends help her recover it before the big game.

Project: Home Run

Objective: The students will enhance their sports knowledge by naming equipment necessary to play various games.

Focus Question: Are there any sports that can be played without equipment?

Directions:

Bring in various sports equipment from home and display. Discuss why each piece of equipment is needed. Use turn wheels to show the equipment for different games. Assemble all the wheels as a class book.

Criterion for Evaluation: Completed turn-wheel book.

Sharing: Read the book to others who are interested in sports.

Another Springboard: *Mice at Bat* by Kelly Oechski. New York: Harper & Row, 1986.

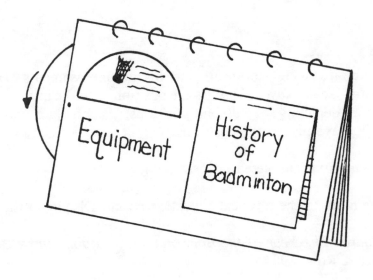

Literature Springboard:

Soccer Sam by Jean Marzollo. New York: Random House, 1987.
    A cousin from Mexico introduces Sam and his friends to the game of soccer.

Project: No Hands

Objective: Students will identify the rules of soccer.

Focus Question: If you were going to teach some friends to play soccer, what rules would you be sure to tell them?

Directions:

    Bring in a soccer ball. Explain the rules of the game and show the game rules outside in slow-motion. Read about the famous soccer player Pelé. Use fold-a-frames to show the soccer rules. Assemble the frames for a book.

Criterion for Evaluation: Completed fold-a-frame book.

Sharing: Read the book to a high school soccer team player. Display in the school library.

Another Springboard: *The Sidewalk Racer and Other Poems of Sports and Motion* by Lillian Morrison. New York: Lothrop, Lee & Shepard, 1977.

Index

This index is comprised of author names, titles of books, and general subjects. Titles that appear in quotation marks refer to specific projects involving paper actions.

About the Authors

Gerry Bohning

Gerry Bohning teaches reading and children's literature courses in the Adrian Dominican School of Education at Barry University, Miami, Florida. She received a B.A. from Dakota Wesleyan University in South Dakota, an M.A. in elementary education from the University of South Dakota, and an Ed.D. in reading from the University of Miami in Florida. Her research interests include the history of pop-up books, and she has published numerous articles on how to use pop-up books in the classroom. Bohning believes in professional networking and is currently an officer with the Florida Reading Association. Her hobbies are crossword puzzles, bicycling, and showing off pictures of her grandchildren.

Ann Phillips

Ann Phillips received her B.S. from Memphis State University and her M.S. from Barry University, Miami. She taught high school social studies in Shelby County, Tennessee, and elementary school in various Dade County (Florida) schools. There she also worked as a certified media specialist. Presently, she is a sixth-grade language arts teacher at Lincoln Park Academy in Fort Pierce, Florida. In addition, she presents workshops on children's literature at local and state conferences. In 1988 Phillips was named Dade County Reading Teacher of the Year. She is married and has two children.

Sandra Bryant

Sandra Bryant was graduated from the University of Florida with a degree in elementary education. She later obtained a master's degree in education from Barry University in Miami, Florida. She currently teaches first grade in Dade County and resides in Homestead, Florida, with her husband Chris and their son Kevin. She enjoys crafts, gardening, and spending time with her family.